LOGANSPORT CASS COUNTY PUBLIC

Y0-CVP-465

BAKER, DAVID   11/30/89
AIRBORNE EARLY WARNING
(7) 1989 J 623.737 BAK S:450229
1501 03 996568 01 8   (IC=0)

B150103996568018B

Military Aircraft Library
Airborne Early Warning

Military Aircraft Library
Airborne Early Warning

DR. DAVID BAKER

**Rourke Enterprises, Inc.
Vero Beach, FL 32964**

© 1989 Rourke Enterprises, Inc.

All rights reserved. No part of this book may be reproduced or utilized in any form or by any means, electronic or mechanical including photocopying, recording or by any information storage and retrieval system without permission in writing from the publisher.

Library of Congress Cataloging-in-Publication Data

Baker, David, 1944-
  Airborne early warning/by David Baker.

  p. cm. — (The Military aircraft series)
  Includes index.
  Summary: Describes how radar and other air surveillance techniques, such as airborne warning and control devices, are used to watch the skies to determine what the enemy is doing.
  ISBN 0-86592-533-X
  1. Electronic warfare aircraft — United States — Juvenile literature 2. Airborne warning and control systems — Juvenile literature. [1. Electronic warfare aircraft.
2. Airplanes, Military. 3. Airborne warning and control systems.]
  I. Title. II. Series: Baker, David, 1944-   Military aircraft Library.
  UG1242.E43B35   1989   88-13769
  623.7'37 — dc19   CIP
                                            AC

CONTENTS

1	Eyes in the Sky	6
2	Radar	14
3	Early Warning	20
4	Sentry	26
5	Command Post	38
	Glossary	46
	Index	48

Eyes in the Sky

When the powered aircraft was invented, many people wondered what use it would be. For centuries, men and women had been trying to get off the earth with varying results. Most of them ended up breaking their necks or deciding that human beings were probably not meant to fly. A few bold pioneers kept working at it, and in December 1903, two bicycle builders from Dayton, Ohio, succeeded in getting their heavier-than-air plane, powered by a small engine, off the ground. The brothers were Wilbur and Orville Wright.

As soon as it proved possible to build a flying machine that could be fully controlled, many people could think of uses for it. An obvious role for the powered flying machine was to move people and things over given distances, such as between two towns or cities. Even the basic *Wright airplane* could reach sufficient speed to get quickly across country. The great benefit, of course, was that the airplane could go in a straight line and did not have to stop for a herd of cattle, like people on the ground had to. Moving things by air required a plane large enough to carry several people or cargo. That would not happen for at least ten years.

Another obvious application of the flying machine was for spying. From a position high above ground, an observer can see great distances and can keep watch on what is happening far away. A person standing on the ground can see about 3 miles. From a height of just over 65 feet, the same person can see 10 miles, and from 35,000 feet the horizon is 230

Lt. Thomas E. Selfridge examines a Wright bi-plane just prior to a test flight in September 1908.

The Wright brothers made the first powered airplane flights in 1903.

In the early part of this century, airships competed with airplanes for military observation duties.

miles away. Of course the human eye cannot actually see things on the ground at that great distance, but the ability to increase one's view with altitude was an obvious advantage.

During the American Civil War of 1861-65, John La Mountain made the first successful aerial reconnaissance by balloon. He had been sent by sea to help General Butler at Fortress Monroe, a Union stronghold. In July 1861, he rose to a height of 1,400 feet and spied on the Confederate camps nearby. Later, he ascended from an armed transport boat in the James River, making the boat, named *Fanny*, the first aircraft carrier.

Later still, La Mountain became the first man to fly over enemy territory when he used light easterly winds to carry his balloon across enemy lines. Dropping ballast to make the balloon lighter, he rose to the level of higher winds blowing west that carried him safely back. Another flyer, Thaddeus Lowe, sent

Balloons in the early part of the twentieth century were used as military observation platforms.

This artist's illustration shows the first flight of a ballon in 1783.

a telegraph message from his balloon after the Battle of Bull Run telling President Lincoln that Washington was not in danger and that "the city, with its girdle of encampments, presents a superb scene."

Several such lessons showed the American military forces the value of powered planes in flying unchallenged across areas of enemy occupation. It took a war to put that experience into action. When World War One began in Europe during August 1914, it created a need for military aviation. At first, balloons were used for spying on the enemy; soon planes, by then sufficiently powerful, were used instead.

The American government had been slow to develop the airplane for war. The military was not prepared, even after three years of fighting in Europe, when America declared war on Germany and came to the aid of the French, the British, the Belgians, and the Italians. All the planes used by U.S. airmen in 1917 and 1918, when peace was restored, were bought from America's allies. That taught the army another lesson: be prepared.

In World War Two, which America joined in 1941, the U.S. was in a better state of readiness. The final lesson, the bitterest of all, was driven home hard on Sunday, December 7, 1941, a day that would live, said President Roosevelt, "in infamy." On that day, the Japanese navy attacked the U.S. naval base at Pearl Harbor, Hawaii. The big lesson learned that day was never forgotten. Peace depends on watching the intentions of a potential enemy as well as being prepared to fight.

Americans learned that a war can be avoided not only by making preparations to fight at a moment's notice but also by knowing exactly what the enemy is up to. In that way, moves can be made to prevent the enemy from even beginning to fight. Early warning is an important part of being prepared. Today, after two world wars, the United States keeps a careful and close watch on potential threats to its security and that of its allies and friends.

In World War One the spy in the sky was a tiny plane made of wood and canvas and a man with a box camera stuck over the side. In World War Two, *radar* played a vital role in detecting enemy aircraft

During the World War One (1914-18), balloons were used extensively to warn troops on the ground of enemy forces approaching the front line.

Early airplanes like this Avro tri-plane were developed as observation platforms and early warning posts.

Observation planes were considered a threat and fighters were designed to shoot them down.

Training devices like this were used to instruct observers on how to use cameras from the air.

A British observation plane swoops low over enemy forces to take back information about troop movements.

and watching when and where his planes were massing for attack. Today, all kinds of electronic devices are employed to watch the skies and provide information about events in the air, at sea, and on the ground.

It is no longer a simple matter of looking out the window of a high-flying airplane or watching a screen for radar blips. Getting useful information means interpreting how the enemy might be trying to hide his real intentions or mask the deployment of some new weapon. Early warning includes spying from outside the enemy's territory, watching his move day and night, scanning the skies constantly for signs of attack, and using electronic sensors to listen to his conversations on radio communication.

Early warning is, however, even more. Where once the air battles were controlled from the ground, they are today increasingly being coordinated from above. *Flying command posts* that link friendly forces receive information about the movements of the enemy and direct the use of surrounding airspace in a form of battle management traffic control. These planes are as important a link in the chain as the fighters and the *interceptors* themselves. Without early warning the information with which to deter the enemy would not be available. Without control of what is going on in the skies, the enemy would gain control of the air and win on the ground.

Radio Waves

Bulbous extensions on the nose of these modified EC-135 planes house large radio and communication equipment.

During World War One, reconnaissance flights were made with nothing more than a camera and a notepad. When radar came along, it added a completely new dimension. No longer were the limitations of the human eye, the camera lens, and bad weather obstacles for learning about what the enemy was doing. Radar works by sending out a signal that is reflected back in various ways by different materials. The word radar stands for **ra**dio **d**etection **a**nd **r**anging.

Radio waves are a form of electromagnetic radiation. Radiation includes things we can see and things we cannot see. Our eyes have developed to allow us a window on only a small portion of the electromagnetic spectrum. We can see visible light but we cannot see *ultra-violet light*, *x-rays*, or *gamma rays*. X-rays are used to probe beneath our skin and show bones in our bodies. They do this because solid substances like bone block the free passage of x-rays. They do not harm us, but they leave a visible image of a skeleton.

Gamma rays are created in *nuclear reactions* and transmitted, or "radiated," by the nucleus of an atom. Gamma rays are released when a nuclear bomb goes off. They are also sent out by violent nuclear reactions going on in the interior of stars far off in the galaxy. Even our own star, the sun, sends out gamma radiation. It is very harmful to all living things, and on earth we are protected by powerful magnetic forces that keep it from penetrating the atmosphere.

Visible light, ultraviolet light, x-rays, and gamma rays lie at one end of the spectrum. At the other lies

Early warning of attacking planes is provided by defense radar on this U.S. Navy destroyer.

infra-red, close to the visible region, and radio waves. Radio waves sent out from a transmitter can be either pulsed or continuous. In *pulsed radar*, continuous bursts of radio energy are transmitted, each one like a tiny package. The speed of radio waves is constant, so by watching the time taken for the package to bounce back, the operator knows the distance between his radar and the object. When the pulse is received back a second pulse is sent, and so on.

In *continuous wave radar* transmissions, on the

The ship's search radar (top) and air track radar (bottom) provide information by which computers control missiles and guns to shoot down incoming enemy aircraft.

other hand, a continuous beam of radio energy is sent out. Instead of transmitting on one frequency, it is sent out on several frequencies at the same time. Radio signals cover a range of frequencies. Commercial radio and TV stations use different frequencies to transmit programs at the same time. A receiver, be it a radio or television set, will respond only to those frequencies the set is tuned to receive. Radio and TV sets have controls and we tune the sets ourselves to receive whichever set of frequencies they are built to pick up.

The continuous wave radar works in a similar way to pulsed radar, but on a continuous basis. The transmitter is constantly moving through a range of frequencies. When the receiver gets the reflected signal back it can measure the distance by noting the time since that particular frequency was sent out. The transmitter and the receiver of either pulsed or continuous wave radar is shaped according to the job it has to do. The radio energy is generated inside the unit and fired at a reflector, or antenna, usually made of wire mesh. The beam bounces off the antenna and is reflected across to the target. It strikes the target, is reflected back to the antenna and analyzed inside the receiver.

The shape of the antenna is designed for a specific role. Search radars continuously watching for signs of enemy aircraft have a broad beam fanning out

Land-based applications of early warning radar give the troops mobile support.

Air attack is a constant threat to ground forces, and wherever they go they must carry early warning radar.

across a wide area. Because the radar set has a specific power level, the strength of a broad-beam signal will be weaker than if it were all concentrated in a narrow beam. It is sufficient, however, for general search purposes. When tracking a specific target, however, narrow-beam antennas are used. Sometimes, several different beam shapes can be sent and received back through the same antenna.

Today all military aircraft carry radar for one purpose or another. Fighters carry radar to watch for enemy planes, to provide information on how far off and how fast the target is flying, and to control the path of rockets and missiles launched to destroy it. Bombers carry radar to warn of attacking fighters and to guide weapons down to their targets on the ground. From the ground, radars watch the skies continuously for signs of activity. This is the fundamental basis of early warning.

Radar on this F-4 Phantom is designed to help it seek out and destroy enemy aircraft.

Radar provides the eyes and ears of combat planes as they seek out enemy aircraft.

Early Warning

The United States uses many devices and systems to watch the skies above, and not all of them can be discussed here. These systems provide the eyes and ears of the nation and would be used to control a suitable response to any level of attack. The first warning of attack by long-range missiles stored in underground silos or underwater submarines would come from spy satellites in orbit 22,300 miles above the earth. At this distance, the satellites keep watch on the surface of the earth below. They are crammed with *infra-red detectors* to observe signs of hot rocket exhausts propelling missiles away from enemy launch positions.

Most radars work by sending out beams in straight lines to get a reflected signal from a solid object. Radio waves do not naturally travel around corners or bend over hills and mountains. They simply pass through or are reflected. Certain high

Early warning of possible missile attack would first be detected by satellites in space.

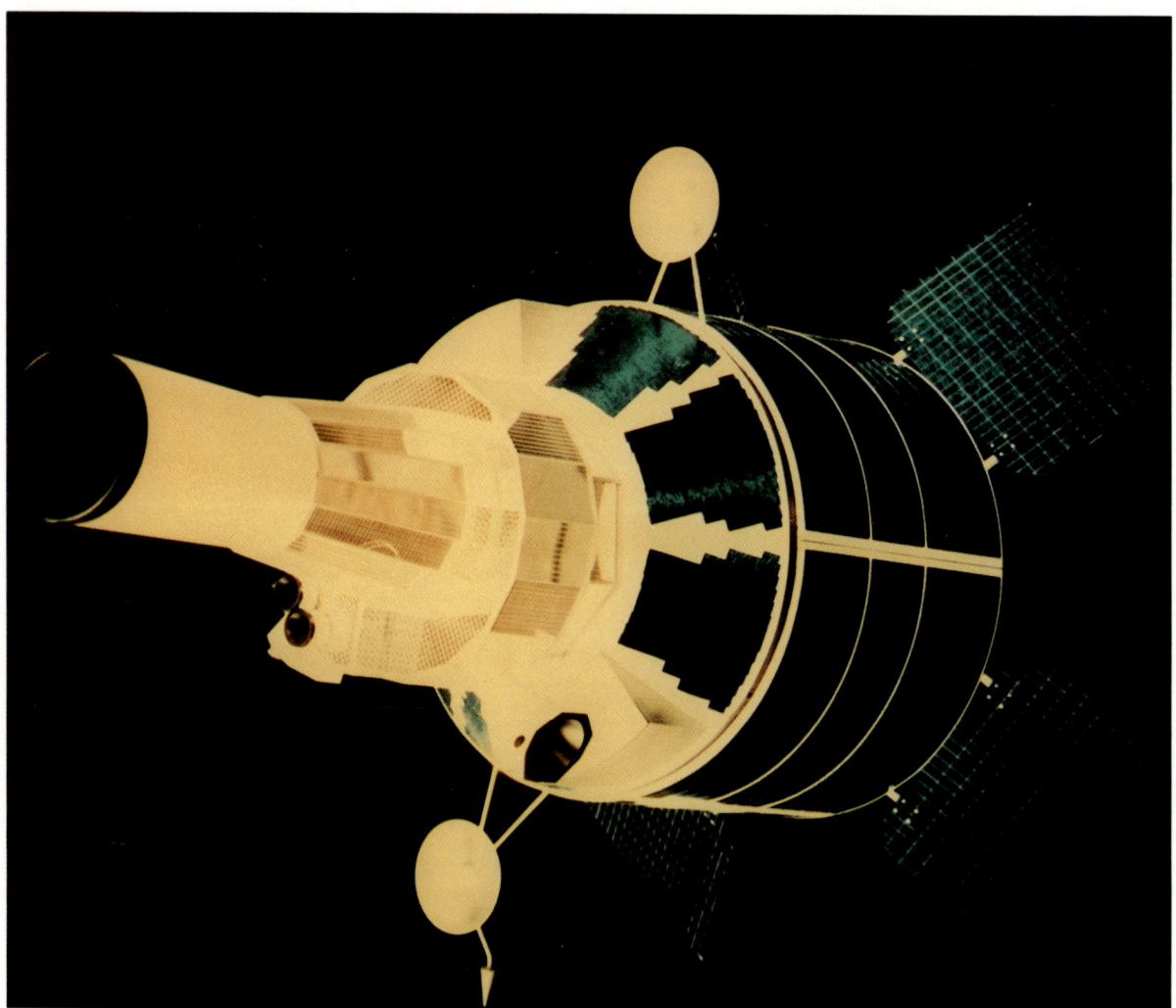

Giant radar installations like this Pave Paws system help protect the United States against surprise attack.

frequencies, however, can be deflected by layers in the earth's upper atmosphere. The *ionosphere*, for instance, will deflect high-frequency radio signals. The ionosphere lies about 120 miles above earth, and when very powerful radio waves are sent toward it they are deflected down at an angle. This kind of deflection is one way to make radio waves "curve."

Radars that operate in this way are called *over-the-horizon (OTH)* radars. The United States is modifying its first line of detection against enemy planes by putting OTH radars in various places across the nation to monitor approaches east, west, and south. The northern boundary and Canada are covered by *Distant Early Warning (DEW)* radar installations in Alaska, Canada, and Greenland.

In use, a powerful OTH radar sends a beam out toward the horizon. It reaches the ionosphere and is deflected down over the curvature of the earth. The signal strikes the ground or any object in between. Aircraft approaching the United States are detected when the return signal follows a reverse route: back up to the ionosphere and down to the antenna that sent it. In this way, aircraft up to 1,800 miles away from the radar can be detected.

OTH radars can give up to an hour's warning time of incoming planes. One hour is enough for fighters to intercept the aircraft and find out whether it intends to be aggressive. The fighter's own radar guides it to its target. Soviet planes routinely challenge the U.S. and her friendly allies in this way. By probing a country's radar installations, planes from another country can learn valuable information about how effective the first country's radar is and how long that country takes to get its fighters into position.

Early warning activities in peacetime are likely to influence the judgment of a potential enemy. A strong early warning system sends a clear and concise message that defenses are always up and that there are no opportunities for conducting a sneak attack without warning. The Soviets try

Designed to track sea-launched ballistic missiles, and occasionally earth satellites, Pave Paws is housed in a giant building 105 feet high.

Deployed in North Dakota, this Safeguard missile defense system seeks out incoming missiles at great range.

Another long-range eye on the sky is this early warning radar system set up at Thule Air Base in Greenland.

continuously to probe the national airspace of western European countries. Each year, Britain's Royal Air Force carries out more than 200 intercepts as Soviet planes probe the defenses.

Radar early warning stations track the Soviet planes and provide information on how many aircraft are coming and where they are heading. Royal Air Force fighters escort the Russian planes away from British territory, and there is usually a friendly exchange. Pilots wave at each other and smile, yet both sides know that if war broke out it would be a deadly game of cat and mouse. The advantage would go to whichever country had the best and most up-to-date intelligence information.

Because radar is the ideal way of "seeing" planes far beyond the range of the human eye in all weathers and conditions, it is not surprising that special planes have been built to carry radar into the air. From a commanding position high above the earth, a single plane can observe activity over several hundred square miles of sky. These planes are alert to everything, from the highest-flying spy

Detected by early warning radars, two United States F-4 Phantoms escort a Soviet bomber away from U.S. naval forces.

Aircraft like this Soviet MiG-29 are equipped with radar that can operate independent of tracking stations in the Soviet Union.

plane to the ground-hugging fighter planes close to the surface of land or sea. From 35,000 feet an aircraft equipped with radar can monitor events up to 230 miles away in any direction.

Because of this, the U.S. Air Force and the U.S. Navy developed a special series of planes designed to carry radar and other electronic sensors for watching large areas where potential enemy activity may suddenly take place. These planes carry powerful radar equipment, and some have rotating antennas sweeping the sky for signs of unidentified planes. They have computers able to process a million operations each second and computer memory banks that store a million words.

Since World War Two, planes that carried surveillance radar and looked for signs of the enemy were called *Airborne Early Warning (AEW)* planes. A new concept has revolutionized AEW, however. This concept expands AEW's task beyond observing enemy planes to coordinating the response to those planes. In other words, the same AEW plane both monitors and controls vast areas of sky. From a single airborne warning plane would come instructions to friendly fighters and attack planes about where the enemy could be found and what to do to destroy him. Carrying out this dual role is the Boeing E-3 Sentry *Airborne Warning and Control System (AWACS)*.

Sentry

The U.S. Air Force has played a leading role since World War Two in developing airborne warning and control systems. The Lockheed EC-121 was operated for many years until it was retired from duty in 1980. This aircraft was a converted Constellation airliner dating back to the 1940s. It had a distinctive set of twin fins on a horizontal tail. The EC-121 was replaced by a derivative of one of the most successful planes since the war, the Boeing Model 367-80. The first aircraft of this type flew in July 1954, when it was intended to be a *cargo/tanker* plane for the air force.

Within a year it was developed into the Boeing 707 airliner, the world's first successful jet passenger plane. It was ordered by the air force as a cargo/tanker plane and entered service in that role during 1957. Major technical developments during the 1960s made it possible for radar to peer over the

The most capable airborne early warning system operated in the world today is carried aboard the Sentry AWACS plane.

Also known as the Boeing E-3, the Sentry is equipped with powerful jet engines that give the plane great range and operational endurance.

horizon and to look down on the ground from above to distinguish low-level objects moving across the surface.

This made the AWACS more effective than ever. Radar was no longer just an extension of human eyes and camera lenses, but it could now locate objects in the air all around it. Development of what is now called *look-down/shoot-down* radar was made possible by the use of advanced electronic equipment. It is one thing to scan the sky and monitor solid objects against a completely neutral background. It is a very different matter to look at objects against trees, leaves, birds, buildings, moving vehicles, and people.

Radar becomes confused when many activities are occurring in the field of view at the same time. Rustling leaves can send a false signal, as can the plume from surf and rough waves. Engineers tackled these problems by designing special signal processors that work like filters to screen out misleading reflections. The advantages of look-down/shoot-down radar are enormous. No aircraft can hide in the surface folds of hills and valleys, because they are being watched from above.

The E-3A carries a special search and tracking radar in the slowly rotating rotodome mounted on top of the fuselage.

Two companies, Hughes and Westinghouse, were contracted to develop *Overland Downlook Radar (ODR)*, and in 1970 Boeing was given the job of building the plane to carry this look down/shoot down device. The familiar Boeing 707 was converted into the first official AWACS plane, called the Boeing E-3 Sentry. Boeing was also given the job of coordinating and integrating all the electronics and radar equipment.

At first Boeing wanted to replace the 707's four jet engines with eight engines of a more advanced type, which would give the plane a longer time in the air and better performance. That idea was dropped, however, and the four engine positions were retained. The Pratt and Whitney engine, delivering 10.5 tons of thrust, is used, as is a new engine that puts out 12 tons of thrust, developed by General Electric and SNECMA, a French company.

The Sentry carries a circular dome on top of two struts mounted above the fuselage just behind the wing. This holds the search radar capable of looking out a distance of 230 miles down to the ground and farther out in mid-air. The circular dome also houses a special radar designed to find out if aircraft in the vicinity are friendly or hostile. It does this by sending out a signal that is picked up by the aircraft in question.

All U.S. aircraft and those of friendly nations carry a special device to acknowledge this signal and say, in effect, "I am a friend." Hostile or enemy aircraft do

Inside Sentry, operators man consoles that scan the skies for several thousand square miles around.

Early warning and command and control aircraft would provide the primary means of coordinating an air response to an unprovoked attack.

The flight crew of an E-3A go through final pre-flight checks.

The E-3A keeps an airborne watch over all air and some ground activity, and provides an ability to coordinate friendly fighters.

not carry this device, and the AWACS plane knows whether or not they are a possible threat by the lack of reaction. The signal frequency and the return message is changed regularly, and an enemy will not know the correct response. Even if an enemy plane tried to outwit the AWACS plane by carrying a special device, he would still not be able to give the appropriate answer.

The flattened dome also carries communications equipment, which the plane uses to keep in touch with a wide range of different people and places.

Scanning a portion of the earth's atmosphere more than 500 miles across, from the surface to an altitude of more than 20 miles, is a heavy responsibility. This vast area could easily include all the airborne activity of an entire conflict. In time of war, instructions from the national command authorities of the United States would flow back and forth between the AWACS plane and wherever the Chiefs of Staff were. Communications would be vital.

The Sentry's equipment consists of many separate communication channels, and no one set of frequencies is used for receiving orders and informing the national leaders of the situation. Communication with the other planes in the area is vital, and many different systems would be used to help friendly planes in and out of the area. In this role, the Sentry is like a giant set of traffic lights in the sky telling planes when to come, when to go, and when to stand and fight the enemy.

Other channels send streams of data about the air situation via satellites to the United States, so that wherever the plane is located it is in constant touch

These men operate as airborne weapons directors who watch consoles that reveal details of enemy air action.

The computer technician's console aboard the E-3 provides detailed information about systems throughout the aircraft.

This airborne radar technician is at his station aboard an E-3, one of many people manning these important aircraft.

33

E-3 planes can be re-fueled in the air to keep them airborne for several days if necessary.

with base and providing continuous information about the situation. With this information, the flow of battle can be controlled locally by the AWACS plane and on a larger scale by the generals and the politicians in the United States. The Sentry can be updated with information and instructions, and it can organize its own replacement in the air when it needs to refuel.

These three functions — search radar, friend or foe identification, and communications — are all contained in the Sentry's dome, which is 30 feet in diameter and 6 feet deep. It is supported on two struts, each 11 feet tall. The dome rotates slowly to scan all directions, and the section that moves weighs 3,395 pounds. During flight to and from its station in the air, the *rotodome* rotates very slowly to keep the bearings lubricated. On station and on alert, the rotodome revolves at a steady six revolutions each minute, or once every 10 seconds.

Of the two companies contracted to develop the radar systems, Westinghouse was successful in bidding for development of the flight equipment. Inside the plane, sophisticated computers feed information to nine separate console positions, each manned during the flight by a specialist electronics engineer. This enables a wide variety of different radar and electronic systems to be used for various mission needs. In some roles, the Sentry would not send out a radio signal but passively listen for tell-tale radar emissions from approaching enemy planes. In this way the enemy would not know the AWACS was in the area and listening to his imminent arrival.

The latest computer equipment carried by the Sentry can perform 1.25 million operations each second. Its memory banks store 665,000 words, which give it enormous capacity for tracking and identifying large numbers of aircraft simultaneously. The entire area being scanned by the rotodome can be divided up into 24 sectors, each one set for a specific type of information. For instance, one type might be the position and range for several enemy aircraft. Another might be the height of various threats in the air. A third could be the detection and identification of ships on the surface of the sea even if they are stationary.

The first E-3 Sentry made its initial flight in October 1975, and the first operational airplane of this type went into service in 1977. A total of 52 Sentry planes have been built, many with special modfications and improvements. The air force makes a continuing effort to add the very latest electronic devices. Improvements in the ability of potential enemies of the U.S. to evade detection

Since it first entered service in 1977, the Boeing E-3A AWACS has won worldwide recognition for its advanced capabilities.

This NKC-135 has been adapted to work as a laser laboratory.

mean that upgrades to the Sentry's electronics are a vital part of staying ahead in the race for technical supremacy.

The aircraft in which the electronic equipment was installed was more than a standard Boeing 707. It, too, had a number of refinements built in over the years. The plane is 152 feet, 11 inches long with a wing span of 145 feet, 9 inches and a height of 41 feet, 9 inches. It has an empty weight of 81 tons and a maximum takeoff weight of 162.5 tons. The E-3 Sentry has a normal cruising speed of 530 MPH, a service ceiling of 29,000 feet, and an endurance on station of 6 hours 1,000 miles from base. With transit time to and from its area of activity, it remains in the air about 10 hours on a normal mission.

The E-3 AWACS plane has also been assigned a role in *NATO*, the North Atlantic Treaty Organization. NATO is a group of 15 countries, including Canada, Iceland, Great Britain, the United States, and 11 countries in Europe. An attack on one of these countries is considered an attack on all 15 countries, and all are pledged to help each other. Serving NATO in this role, the Sentry keeps guard on the western world.

The E-3 Sentry was developed from the KC-135 tanker plane, as was this version for long-range communication.

Command Post

There is one special AWACS plane operated by the navy and carried on every U.S. aircraft carrier afloat. Built by Grumman and called the E-2 Hawkeye, it has a rotating, circular dome like the E-3 and maintains watch from high above the sea on aircraft coming and going to and from the carrier. More important, it serves as an early warning system and controls and coordinates fighters launched from the carrier to attack the enemy.

The Hawkeye is 57 feet, 6 inches in length and has a wing span of 80 feet, 7 inches. From a height of 30,000 feet, it surveys airspace for 300 miles in all directions. Hawkeye's rotating dome works on exactly the same principles as the E-3 Sentry's. Large aircraft can be seen up to 290 miles away, small planes at 230 miles, and tiny *cruise missiles* racing over the waves at 115 miles. The radar can track and identify up to 250 targets at the same time and control more than 30 interceptions between friendly fighters and enemy targets. In every sense, the Hawkeye is both AWACS and *airborne command post*. It receives instructions from the carrier below, but it coordinates the attack alone. Because it is controlling many fighters going after several different types of targets, it can organize its own defense. Hawkeye does this by temporarily

The Grumman E-2C Hawkeye operates as the main early warning eyes for the air fleet at sea.

Hawkeye operates regularly on and off the carrier deck, watching the skies far beyond the horizon.

The E-2C has folding wings to limit the space it needs aboard crowded carrier decks.

Boeing employees and visitors inspect the prototype E-6A TACAMO during its public unveiling in December 1986.

The air control officer's work station inside the E-2C Hawkeye.

Produced at the Boeing Renton, Washington, factory, the E-6 is based on the KC-135 and Boeing 707 airliner.

diverting friendly warplanes to its aid should any enemy fighters or missiles threaten its own survival.

In all, the navy has 95 Hawkeyes, and a typical carrier has four planes of this type, each able to control two squadrons of fighters in the air. The navy is always eager to point out the economics of operating its AWACS compared with the air force's E-3 Sentry. While costing only half of what the Sentry costs, the Hawkeye can do a similar job, although it can coordinate fewer friendly planes simultaneously.

The increasing reliance on AWACS planes has taken the old business of watching the enemy to heights unimagined when balloon pilots spied on Confederate troops more than 120 years ago. The awesome power of modern weapons, controlled and coordinated by planes like the E-3 and the E-2, places tremendous responsibility on these planes.

Providing accurate information about potential action by enemy planes as quickly as possible is crucial to a country's defense system. The transformation from airborne early warning to airborne warning and control concepts has inspired yet another type of aircraft: the airborne command post. Through this command post, supervision and coordination of vast resources are brought under one authority.

The navy developed the concept of a survivable

Submarine communications crew members operate this ground-based E-6A training device.

airborne communications and command system for its submarine fleet. They first used a propeller-driven Lockheed EC-130 aircraft, which was good but limited by its performance. The EC-130's replacement was yet another variation of the old Boeing 707. The navy had Boeing adapt the basic E-3 Sentry for their own unique needs. The first one flew in 1987, and production of 15 planes began in 1988, with completion of the order expected by 1993.

The navy command post is called the E-6A and comes without the familiar rotodome of the air force E-3. The E-6A's primary role is to communicate instructions to the expanding fleet of Trident *ballistic-missile submarines* of the Ohio class. These missiles are the most powerful in the navy and stand as a strategic nuclear deterrent of vital national importance. The difficulty of communicating with

Long-range airborne early warning planes can be kept in the air for long periods by re-fueling them from KC-10 tanker planes.

submerged submarines calls for special devices; a dedicated plane is necessary to ensure continuous communication when necessary.

The E-6A is basically the same size as the E-3, but it has a maximum takeoff weight of 171 tons. The E-6A can fly just over 7,000 miles without refueling, and it has a normal endurance of 10 hours, 30 minutes on station about 1,000 miles from base. With several in-flight refuelings, the plane can remain airborne for 72 hours. The aircraft has been given the name *TACAMO* from "Take Charge And Move Out," the instructions that would be sent to submarines in the event of sudden war triggered by a surprise attack.

Because the air force would need to coordinate numerous operations in wartime from a position of safety, Boeing has built four special versions of their 747 Jumbo Jet airliner. Called E-4 advanced airborne command posts, these planes would carry the Chiefs of Staff into the air. From there they would command the battle or the war. The plane can accommodate a large battle staff and has a conference room, communications center, and rest area. It has provision for aerial refueling and

Command and control of United States forces in war time would be carried out by high-ranking officers on board E-4B aircraft.

The KC-10 extends the range and endurance of airborne early warning aircraft.

computers to help the generals and the President decide the weapons that should be used in response to an attack.

Periodically refueled in the air by a Lockheed KC-10 Extender or a Boeing KC-135 tanker, the E-4 could remain airborne for up to three full days if necessary. The plane is equipped with every device necessary to maintain full contact with missile forces in their silos, large bomber forces in the air awaiting their targets and destinations, armies on the ground gathering to turn back an assault, or squadrons of fighters converging on enemy targets.

The action controlled by the battle staff aboard the E-4 could involve every continent on earth and millions of fighting men and women in many countries. Linked by satellites to local commanders, the E-4 is the nerve center for deciding what to do and how to fight. It then communicates those instructions to the right people in the right places.

In addition to the four E-4 aircraft for strategic command and control, the air force operates 21 older EC-135 planes that can perform a similar job. In wartime, they would be linked to the E-4 to relay instructions to regional battle units. The E-4 and EC-135 forces would be used only in the event of a major war on a colossal scale. Still, they are a very long way from a man in a wood-and-canvas plane, carrying a camera.

GLOSSARY

Airborne command post	An aircraft sent up to control and coordinate many different types of friendly aircraft involved in an air battle.
Airborne Early Warning (AEW)	The use of aircraft to detect surprise attack from hostile aircraft by locating them on long range radar sets.
Airborne Warning and Control Systems (AWACS)	An aircraft used to detect hostile attack and to control the response of friendly forces against those incoming planes.
Ballistic-missile submarine	A submarine carrying nuclear-tipped ballistic missiles, which are capable of attacking targets on land or at sea across intercontinental distances.
Cargo/tanker	Aircraft with the dual role of carrying freight and refueling other aircraft in the air.
Continuous wave radar	A beam of radio energy sent out in a continuous manner, unlike pulsed radar, which is sent out in bursts.
Cruise missiles	Missiles designed to fly like small pilotless aircraft, usually across great distances, and attack targets on land or at sea.
Distant Early Warning (DEW)	A series of radar installations set up to detect unexpected attack with antennas in Alaska, Canada, and Greenland.
Flying command posts	Aircraft carrying high-ranking officers who receive information about movements of the enemy and direct the use of air forces in a battle or war.
Gamma rays	High intensity radiation produced in great bursts in the universe and in violent nuclear explosions.
Infra-red	Radiation of the electromagnetic spectrum just outside the band of visible light.
Infra-red detectors	Devices attached to aircraft or missiles to observe signs of hot rocket exhausts by picking up the infra-red emissions from their heat.
Interceptors	Fighter planes designed to attack approaching enemy aircraft.
Ionosphere	A layer in the very thin upper atmosphere approximately 120 miles high that deflects certain high-frequency radio signals.
Look-down/shoot-down radar	Radar units designed to look down at low-flying aircraft or helicopters and detect them against the background of the earth's surface.
North Atlantic Treaty Organization (NATO)	An alliance of the U.S., Canada, and 11 West European countries operating under a military pact to support one another; an attack on one is considered an attack on all.
Nuclear reactions	The act of fusing atomic particles together, thereby liberating enormous quantities of energy. Nuclear reactions occur in the core of the sun and in nuclear explosions.

Over-the-horizon radar (OTH)	Radar that seems to bend around the curvature of the earth by bouncing off the ionosphere.
Overland Downlook Radar (ODR)	Radar operated from a high-flying aircraft to look down at the ground over great distances and pick up and track the movement of aircraft.
Pulsed radar	Bursts of radio energy interspersed with brief pauses.
Radar	**Ra**dio **D**etection **A**nd **R**anging. A system of detecting objects by bouncing radio signals off them.
Rotodome	The rotating, circular dome housing special radar equipment and mounted on the top of an early warning aircraft to detect enemy planes at great range.
TACAMO	**Ta**ke **C**harge **a**nd **M**ove **O**ut. The name given to the E-6A aircraft which coordinates and communicates instructions to the fleet of ballistic missile submarines operated by the United States Navy.
Ultra-violet light	Radiation harmful to humans produced naturally by nuclear reactions occurring in the core of the sun and artificially produced on earth.
Wright airplane	This plane, built by the Wright brothers in 1903, was the first powered heavier-than-air machine to be successfully flown.
X-ray	Radiation produced in nuclear reactions and artificially produced on earth, particularly in medical applications for observing the bones of a human skeleton.

INDEX

Page references in *italics* indicate photographs or illustrations.

airborne command post	38, 41, 44	La Mountain, John	8
Airborne Warning and Control System (AWACS)	25, *27*, 28, 31, 34, 35, 36, 38, 41	Lincoln, President	10
		Lockheed: EC-121	26
		EC-130	42
American Civil War	8	KC-10 Extender	*43, 45*
Avro tri-plane	*11*	look-down/shoot-down radar	27
Boeing: E-3 Sentry	25, *26, 27*, 28, *29, 30, 31*, 32, *33, 34, 35*, 36, *37*, 38, 41, 42, 44	MiG-29	*25*
		NATO	36
		NKC-135	*36*
KC-135	45		
Model 367-80	26	Ohio-class ballistic-missile submarine	42
707	26, 28, 36, 42	over-the-horizon (OTH) radar	21
747 Jumbo Jet	44	overland downlook radar (ODR)	28
Butler, General	8		
Constellation	26	Pave Paws	*21, 23*
cruise missile	38	Phantom	*19, 24*
		Pratt and Whitney	28
Distant Early Warning (DEW) radar	21	Roosevelt, President	10
E-2 Hawkeye	*38, 39, 40,* 41	Safeguard	*22*
E-3 Sentry	25, *26, 27*, 28, *29, 30, 31*, 32, *33, 34, 35*, 36, *37*, 38, 41, 42, 44	Sentry	25, *26, 27*, 28, *29, 30, 31*, 32, *33, 34, 35*, 36, *37*, 38, 41, 42, 44
E-4	44, 45	SNECMA	28
E-4B	*44*		
E-6A	*40, 41, 42,* 44	TACAMO	44
EC-121	26	Trident	42
EC-130	42		
EC-135	*14,* 45	Westinghouse	28, 34
Extender	*43, 45*	World War One	10, 14
		World War Two	10, 25, 26
F-4 Phantom	*19, 24*	Wright airplane	*6*
		Wright, Wilbur and Orville	6, *7*
General Electric	28		
Grumman E-2 Hawkeye	38, 39, 40, 41		
Hawkeye	*38, 39, 40,* 41		
Hughes	28		
Jumbo Jet	44		
KC-10 Extender	*43, 45*		
KC-135	45		